Computer

Basics

Ron Greener

Computer Services

Table of Contents

Computer Services

Parts of a Computer

Clock (2 GHz)

Controls speed of microprocessorAdvertised: 2GHz

(2,000,000,000 instructions per second)

Display

Gets bytes from memory

Keyboard

Typing sends bytes to memory

Mouse

ends signals to memory for communicating with the microprocessor

Printer

Receives bytes from memory for printing characters and graphics

Microprocessor

Central piece of hardware.

20 million transistors

Purpose: execute program instructions

Advertised: Pentium or AMD

Memory

RAM (Random Access Memory)

Purpose: Temporary Storage for Programs and data files. Programs must be transferred from the Hard Disk into memory in order to run

Advertised: 512MB (512,000,000) byte locations)

Very important to have at least 512MB for good performance

CD-RW

Removable storage for programs, data files, pictures, songs. Referred to as a "burner" because of the laser beam recording.

Flash Disk

Replacement for floppy disks. Removable storage for saving programs, data files, pictures, songs.

Hard Disk

Purpose: Permanent storage for programs and data files, that is, Windows, Word, Excel, Internet Explorer, pictures, songs, letters, reports, etc

Advertised: 130GB

130GB= 130,000,000,000 Byte locations

Modem

Converts bytes from memory into analog signals for communicating to the Internet

Internet

Computer Services

Computer Basics

SIX THINGS THAT THE MOUSE CAN DO. The mouse is a device that is used to perform tasks that we do on the computer. It is what allows us to talk to the computer and tell it what to do. For instance, we use the mouse to click on tiny pictures called icons to start up programs such as Solitaire or Word or the Internet Explorer. The mouse is made up of 2 buttons; the left mouse button and the right mouse button. There are four tasks that the left can do and two for the right button.

Left Mouse Tasks:

1. <u>Point</u>: moving the mouse so as to position it on an object such as the Start button.

2. <u>Click</u>: One click on an object using the left mouse button

3. <u>Double Click</u>: Two quick clicks of the left mouse button

4. <u>Drag</u>: Holding down the left mouse and then moving the pointer to a new location

Right Mouse Tasks:

1. <u>Right-Click</u>: Causes a list of useful commands to open

2. <u>Right-Drag</u>: Hold down the right mouse, move the pointer to a new location, choose from a list of commands that appear.

Double-clicking a desktop icon, opens the program for that icon

Right-clicking a desktop icon, provides a list of useful commands

Computer Services

Computer Basics

Parts of a Window

When any program is opened (started), then it is referred to as an open window. They have a somewhat consistent appearance to them. The diagram below shows the My Computer program opened and "restored down" from the maximized view so that the Windows desktop can be identified as well.

Parts of a Window

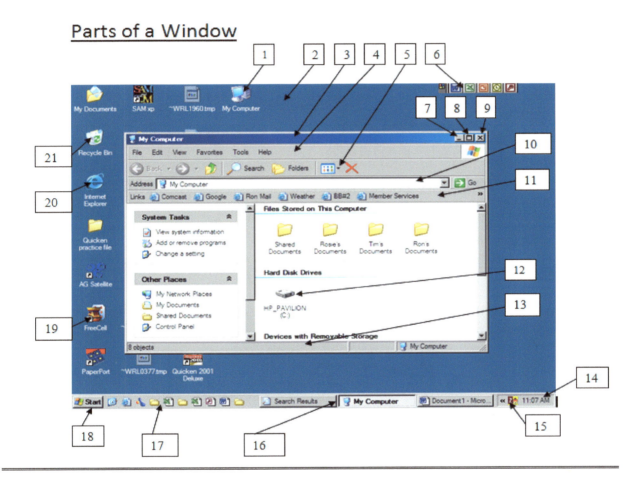

1. My Computer icon	12. Hard drive icon
2. Desktop	13. My Computer Status bar
3. My Computer Title bar	14. Clock
4. Menu bar	15. Tray/Notification area
5. Standard buttons toolbar	16. Task bar
6. Office toolbar	17. Quick launch toolbar
7. Minimize button	18. Start button
8. Maximize button	19. Desktop Shortcut
9. Close button	20. IE icon
10. Address window	21. Recycle bin icon
11. Links toolbar	

Computer Basics

Checking System Resources

Checking System Resources (Windows XP)

1. Right click My Computer
2. Click Properties
3. Click the General tab
4. Note the:
- Version of Windows
- Service Pack 3
- Type of Processor
- Clock speed (Hz value)
- The amount of RAM

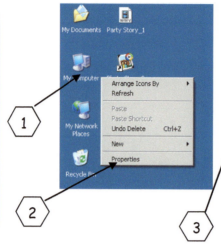

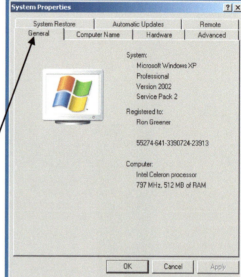

Checking System Resources (Windows Vista & 7)

1. Click Start
2. Right click Computer
3. Click Properties
4. Note the:
- Version of Windows
- Service Pack 2
- Type of Processor
- Clock speed (Hz value)
- The amount of RAM (memory).

Computer Services

Computer Basics

Hard Disk Usage

Checking Hard Disk Usage

1. Double-click My Computer.
2. Right-click Local Disk (C:).
3. Click Properties.
4. Note the bytes of Used, Free, and Capacity.

1

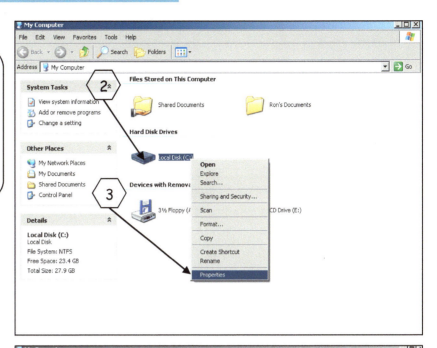

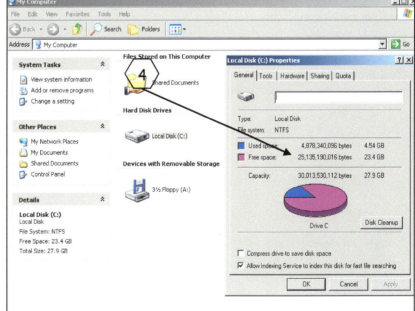

Computer Services

Computer Basics

Disk Cleanup

Disk Cleanup is a Windows maintenance utility that provides for the removing of unneeded files that have built up on your hard disk. Running this task frees up hard disk space and provides the potential for improving overall performance. Run this once per month and preferably prior to doing a defragment.

Performing a Disk Cleanup

1. Perform the steps in "Hard Disk Usage" (pg. 11) to get the Local Disk Properties window.
2. Click the Disk Cleanup button
3. Observe the "calculating"
4. Check the 4 items shown (these 4 have always been good choices, the others are done at your discretion).
5. Click OK, then Yes, and observe the progress of the cleaning.

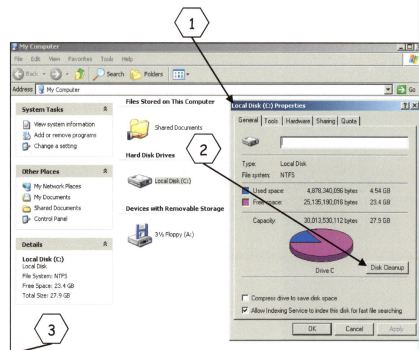

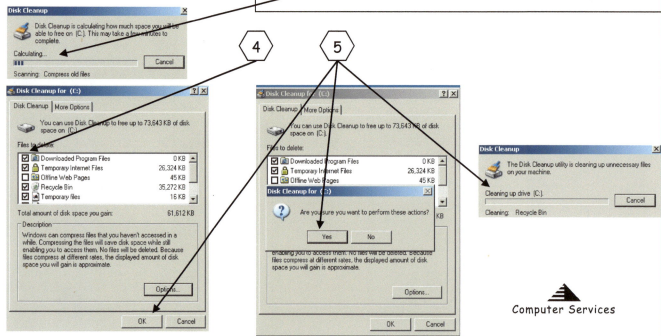

Computer Services

8

Computer Basics

Proper Shutdown of Your Computer

It is very important that your computer be shutdown properly. The reason behind the importance is that Windows has opened many files from the Hard Disk and transferred copies of them into the computer's memory. Prior to shutting down power, Windows needs to close those files plus do some additional house-keeping tasks. Should it not get the opportunity to do so, then when your computer is started back up, Windows is very confused by the condition of those files and finds it necessary to fix them before running your computer. Sometimes this is a rather insignificant problem and easily corrected by Windows. But depending on the situation, it can be a serious problem. In that case Windows runs special software like Checkdisk in an attempt to correct the problem. Another big reason to cycle down using the Shut Down command, is that some updates that have been downloaded from Microsoft, require that they be installed during the Shut Down cycle. So bottom line, does a lot of housekeeping that is a very healthy experience for your computer.

To Shut Down:

1. Click the Start button

2. Click Turn Off Computer (Vista, the black arrow)

3. Click Turn Off (Vista, Shut Down)

4. Allow the computer to cycle down and turn off power automatically

5. **_Note_** that this procedure can be used to Restart (reboot) which means loading a fresh copy of Windows into the computer's memory. This causes the computer to go through the same cycle down as Shut Down except that it does not power off, but instead, powers back up.

6. **_Note_** that Stand By does **_not_** cause the cycle down to occur, but just puts the computer into a reduced power state.

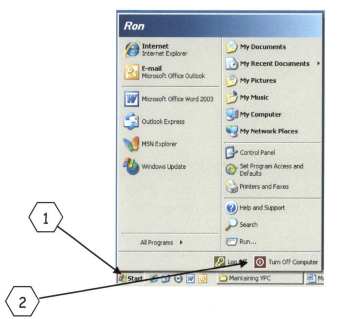

Is it OK to leave my computer on all of the time?

Answer: NO

The power down cycle provides:

1. Housekeeping

2. Installation of updates

3. Closes the door on hackers

4. Less prone to corruption due to power surges

9

Computer Basics

Using the My Computer Program

Using My Computer

My Computer is a program that is used for displaying the contents of disk drives. It could be a case where you have just saved a file or folder to your removable Flash Disk so that you can transfer it to your work computer. You want to verify that the file is really saved there. Or maybe you've just done a backup of the My Documents folder and you want to verify that an exact copy of the My Documents has been saved on your External Hard Disk.

This procedure is demon-strated by using a Flash Disk. However, it could be the Hard Disk (C:), or the CD disk as well.

1. Insert a Flash Disk into any USB port.

2. Close out of any windows that popup.

3. Click the Start button

4. Click My Computer

5. Double-click the removable device icon that represents your Flash Disk.

6. The window that opens shows the contents of the Flash Disk.

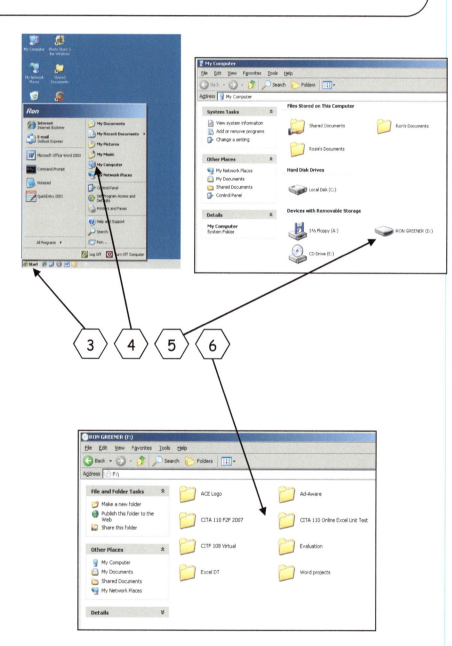

Computer Services

Anti-Virus Protection

Computer viruses are programs written by highly skilled individuals who are seeking fame and bragging rights. Viruses find their way into your computer through the Internet meaning email, and the downloading of webpage content. Once into your computer, they spread, use valuable resources, cause your computer to run slow, and in some cases do damage to the point of requiring total recovery of the hard disk. Obviously it is extremely important to have an anti-virus program installed, up to date, and always running in the background.

When you purchase protection for your computer, be certain to select an "Internet Security" package which includes anti-virus, anti-spyware, and a firewall. PC-Cillin is recommended due to experience, but Norton and McAfee are also well recognized products.

Note that *PC-Cillin Internet Security* is running on this computer. The presence of the PC-Cillin capsule in the lower right corner of your desktop, indicates that it is running in the background all of the time. Double-click to open the information panel shown below. The date shown in "Last Update" indicates when the most current definition files have been downloaded from the provider. These programs are written so that they will do automatic updates. Therefore, that date should be checked periodically for being not more than 2 days old. This ensures that your subscription (typically 1 year) is still valid and the protection is current.

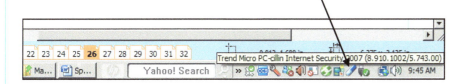

Shows the results of a scan of the hard drive. Select all and remove.

Important date

Computer Services

Word Basics

Computer Services

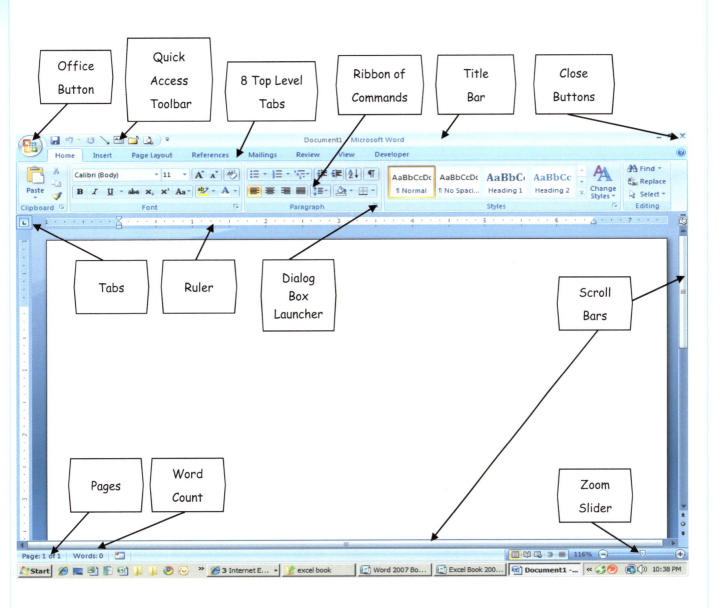

Office Button

Quick Access Toolbar

8 Top Level Tabs

Ribbon of Commands

Title Bar

Close Buttons

Tabs

Ruler

Dialog Box Launcher

Scroll Bars

Pages

Word Count

Zoom Slider

Computer Services

Microsoft Word 2007/10

Setting Margins

Margins are those areas on the top, bottom, left and right sides that are reserved for white space. The exception to this is that enclosed within the top and bottom margins are header and footer areas which are meant to be used for page numbering and other such content that is to be repeated on every page of a multi-page document. In addition to making the printed page more presentable, changing the margins should be considered when attempting to squeeze more content onto a page(s) thereby creating the potential for reducing the number of printed pages.

Setting Margins

1. Click the Page Layout tab

2. Click margins

3. Select one of the presets or select Custom Margins to adjust otherwise.

4. For Custom Margins, the Page Setup dialog box allows for setting to specified values.

NOTE: GUTTER is the binding area of a book.

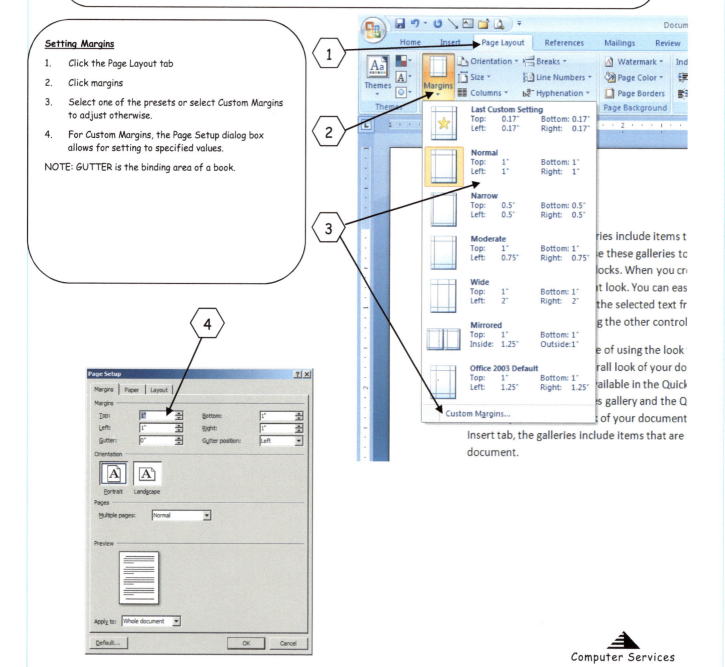

Computer Services

Setting Orientation

Orientation refers to setting up the page for portrait (8 1/2 wide by 11 high) or landscape (11 wide by 8 1/2 high). Portrait is more normal but occasionally the document lends itself to being wider than it is tall.

Setting Orientation

1. Click the Page Layout tab

2. Click orientation

3. Select Landscape or Portrait

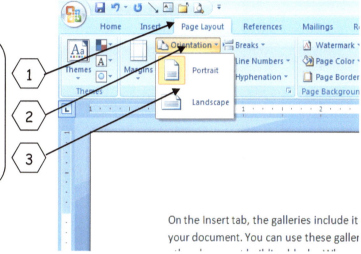

On the Insert tab, the galleries include it
your document. You can use these galler

Portrait

Landscape

Computer Services

Selecting (highlighting) Text

Selecting text is the process of causing it to be highlighted. It is the first step in formatting text. Whatever is highlighted is then changed when formatting commands such as font, font size, font color, bold, italicize, underline, centering, etc. are clicked. Dragging thru text with the left mouse is the most basic way of highlighting. This page describes ways which are faster and more accurate.

On the Insert tab, the galleries include items that are designed to coordinat your document. You can use these galleries to insert tables, headers, footer other document building blocks. When you create pictures, charts, or diagr with your current document look. You can easily change the formatting of s

> Select a **word** by double clicking on it.

On the insert tab, the galleries include items that are designed to coordinate with the overall look of your document. You can use these galleries to insert tables, headers, footers, lists, cover pages, and other document building blocks. When you create pictures, charts, or diagrams, they also coordinate with your current document look. You can easily change the formatting of selected text in the document text by choosing a look for the selected text from the Quick Styles gallery on the Home tab. You can also format text directly by using the other controls on the Home tab.¶

Most controls offer a choice of using the look from the current theme or using a format that you specify directly. To change the overall look of your document, choose new Theme elements on the Page Layout

> Select a **paragraph** by triple clicking on it.

On the Insert tab, the galleries include items that are designed to coordinate with the overall look of your document. You can use these galleries to insert tables, headers, footers, lists, cover pages, and other document building blocks. When you create pictures, charts, or diagrams, they also coordinate with your current document look. You can easily change the formatting of selected text in the document text by choosing a look for the selected text from the Quick Styles gallery on the Home tab. You can also format text directly by using the other controls on the Home tab.¶

> Select a **sentence** by holding down the CTRL key and clicking in the sentence.

On the Insert tab, the galleries include items that are designed to coordinate with the overall look of your document. You can use these galleries to insert tables, headers, footers, lists, cover pages, and other document building blocks. When you create pictures, charts, or diagrams, they also coordinate with your current document look. You can easily change the formatting of selected text in the document text by choosing a look for the selected text from the Quick Styles gallery on the Home tab. You can also format text directly by using the other controls on the Home tab.¶

Most controls offer a choice of using the look from the current theme or using a format that you specify directly. To change the overall look of your document, choose new Theme elements on the Page Layout tab. To change the looks available in the Quick Style gallery, use the Change Current Quick Style Set command. Both the Themes gallery and the Quick Styles gallery provide reset commands so that you can always restore the look of your document to the original contained in your current template. On the Insert tab, the galleries include items that are designed to coordinate with the overall look of your document.¶

¶

> Select an **entire document** by holding down the **CTRL** key and then tap the **A** key on the keyboard.

On the insert tab, the galleries include items that are designed to coordinate with the overall lo your document. You can use these galleries to insert tables, headers, footers, lists, cover pages other document building blocks. When you create pictures, charts, or diagrams, they also coord with your current document look. You can easily change the formatting of selected text in the do text by choosing a look for the selected text from the Quick Styles gallery on the Home tab. You format text directly by using the other controls on the Home tab.¶

> Select **lines** by clicking in the left margin.

Most controls offer a choice of using the look from the current theme or using a format that you specify directly. To change the overall look of your document, choose new Theme elements on the Page Layout tab. To change the looks available in the Quick Style gallery, use the Change Current Quick Style Set command. Both the Themes gallery and the Quick Styles gallery provide reset commands so that you can always restore the look of your document to the original contained in your current template. On the Insert tab, the galleries include items that are designed to coordinate with the overall look of your document.¶

> **De-select** by clicking in the right margin white space.

NOTEs: (1) Use the CTRL key to select non-adjacent areas.

Microsoft Word 2007/10

Formatting Selected Text

On the previous page, many methods of selecting text were shown. Selected text can then be formatted. Most of the formatting commands appear in the ribbon of the Home tab. Shown below are samples of text that has been first selected and then a format applied.

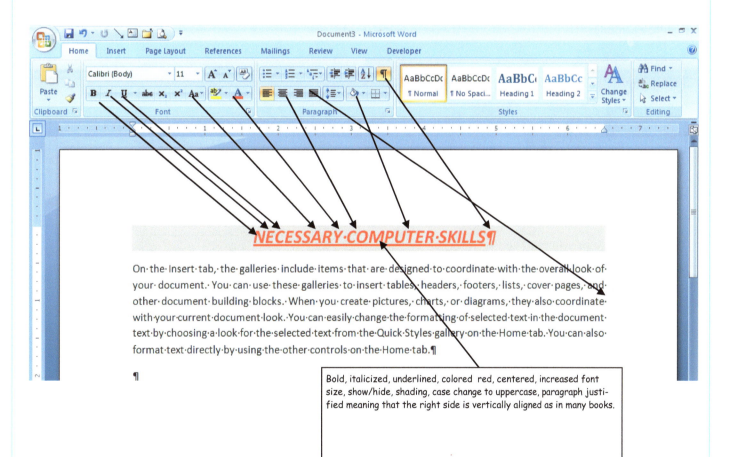

Bold, italicized, underlined, colored red, centered, increased font size, show/hide, shading, case change to uppercase, paragraph justified meaning that the right side is vertically aligned as in many books.

Computer Services

Microsoft Word 2003/10

Block Style Business Letter

2" for header

Ron Greener

5832 Oak Creek Lane

Brighton, MI 48116 (2" for letter-
head)

February 2, 2009

(2 line spaces)

- Block style business letter, all components begin flush with the left mar-gin.
- Font: Calibri, 11
- Single line spacing

John Gray

1654 Bayshore Drive

Muskegon, MI 49115

Dear John,

This is to inform you that we have ac-
cepted your bid for the purchase of 250
desktop computers. It is our under-
standing that you will deliver and install
them at a cost to us of $25,000 payable
the completion of the installation and
testing. We expect to be up and running by March 10, 2009.

NOTE: For the Modified Block Style Business Letter, the date, complementary close, and signature lines are tabbed over to 1/2" to the right of center.

at

Should you have questions, please contact me at 810-227-8385.

Computer Services

Saving a Word File

Saving a document is the process of transferring a copy of the Word document which has been created in the computer's memory as a file, to the hard disk which is a permanent storage area. This is done so that when the computer is powered off, the document is not lost since it has been recorded magnetically on the hard disk. The Save As command is required for the first save so that a file name and a folder location can be specified. Saving thereafter is done by just the Save command. Note that saving should be done frequently while working on a document so that in the case of a power failure or computer lock-up, your work will not be lost.

Saving Your File

1. Click the Office button
2. Point to Save As
3. Click on Word Document
4. Type in a file name
5. Click Documents (or My Documents)
6. Click New Folder
7. Enter a name in the folder window.
8. Tap the Enter key on the keyboard
9. Click Save

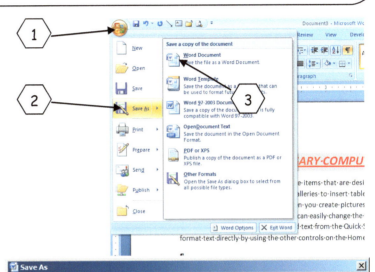

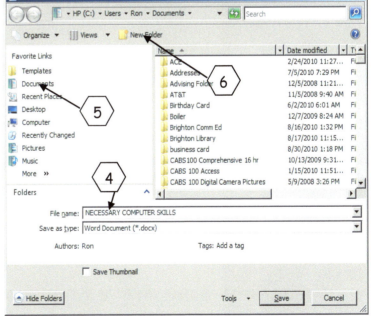

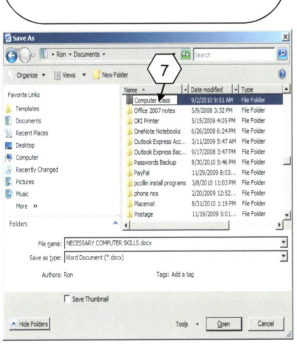

Computer Services

Microsoft Word 2007/10

Opening a Saved File

A document that has been saved to the Hard Disk, can at a later time, be opened for purposes of editing, printing, saving to a different location, or giving it a new name. Opening means to transfer a copy of it from the Hard Disk to computer memory. The important fact to understand is that all files on a computer, Word or otherwise, when double clicked will open and present themselves in the application (program) in which they were created. So double clicking a Word file icon, first of all causes the Word program to open and then the Word file to open in the Word program.

Opening a File

1.   Click the Start button (lower left corner of Desktop)
2.   Click Documents (or My Documents Windows XP).
3.   Double click the folder of interest
4.   Double click the file of interest
5.   Note the file is opened in Word

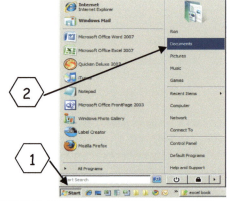

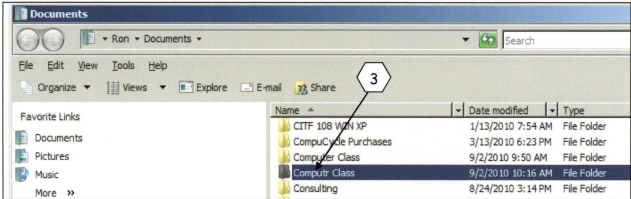

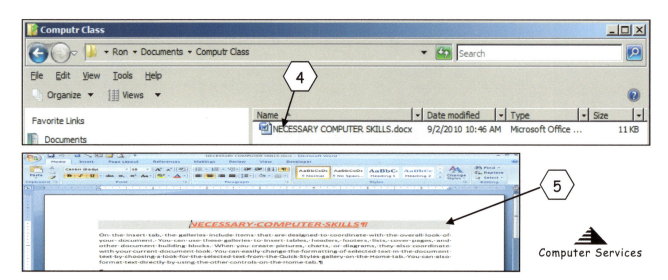

Computer Services

Inserting Clipart

Word comes with graphical images called clipart that can be inserted into a document so as to make it more interesting and appealing. You ask for clipart by entering a keyword into a search box. Word returns a list that has been retrieved from both the hard disk of your computer and from a Microsoft website. Finding one that is appropriate and then clicking on it, causes the image to be inserted into the document at the location where the cursor is located. Sizing handles (dots) appear on the borders which are used to change the size of the image.

Inserting Clipart

1. With the mouse, click the cursor at the desired location in the document.

2. Click the Insert tab.

3. Click Clipart in the "illustrations" group

4. Type a keyword into the search for box

5. Click GO

6. Click on the clipart image of your choice.

7. Note that it has been inserted into the document at the location of the cursor.

8. Alternately click the image and then white space and notice that it becomes selected and de-selected.

9. Notice that when the clipart is selected, a contextual tab appears that causes special graphical commands to appear on the ribbon.

10. Click the Home tab and then the center command button to center the clipart.

11. Place the mouse on any one of the 8 white dots and drag in/out to resize the graphic

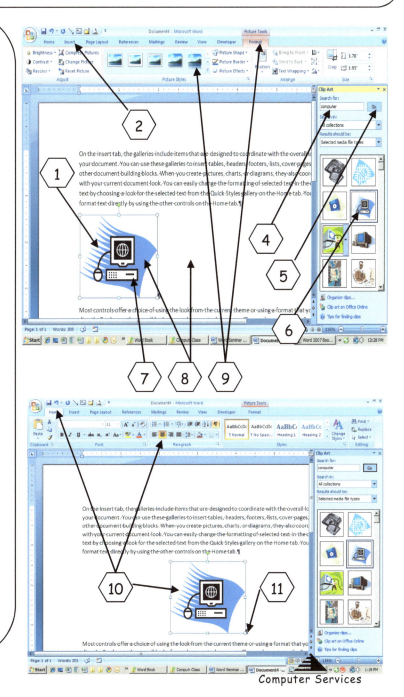

Computer Services

Microsoft Word 2007/10

Undo and Redo

The Undo command allows you to retract commands that have been done. This is used when the task does not accomplish the intended result. More often than not, this is a better choice that trying to fix the wrongdoing. Redo on the other hand lets you change your mind about the undoing and go back to the point where you began undoing (undoes the undoing). You can undo everything back to the start of the document. However, once you close out and then open again, the ability to undo from that point is gone. Only future tasks can then be undone.

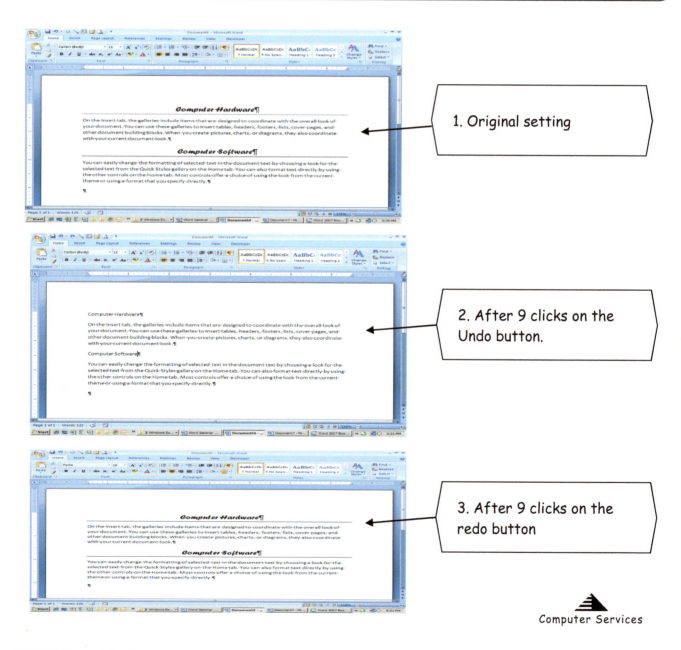

1. Original setting

2. After 9 clicks on the Undo button.

3. After 9 clicks on the redo button

Computer Services

Spell Checker. Word puts a red wavy underline under each word that it cannot find a match for in its spelling dictionary. Most of the time this means a spelling error. However, in the case of a proper name, you have to judge for yourself as to the correct spelling. Right-clicking those designated as spelling errors, provides a list of possible correct spellings that can be clicked to replace the designated word. Proofreading is especially important since some words may be spelled correctly but are out of context such as *hear* instead of *here* or *wit* instead of *with*, good spellings that would not be flagged as errors.

Right clicking Sence produces a list of possible good spellings to pick from

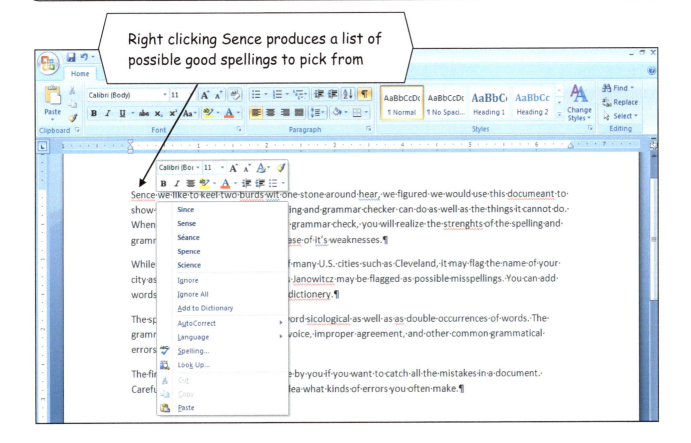

Computer Services

Energy Star Announcement. Refer to the next page that shows the outcome of the instructions below.

1. Enable the **show/hide** feature.

2. **Type** in the document below....allow word wrap

3. Set the left and right **margins** to 2 inches

4. Check for & correct **spelling errors (red wavy underlines)**

5. **Word count**: words _____characters
   _____lines_____

6. Change the **font** to **size 12, arial black** for the entire document.

7. Add **bullets** to the **two lines** under the "**LOOK FOR**"... heading

8. **Center** the two headings "**PRACTICE GREEN**"... and "**LOOK FOR**"...

9. **Change** the **font size** for the two **headings** to **14**

10. **Underline** <u>one year</u>.

11. Set the **paragraph** beginning with **The goal of** to **full justification**.

12. **Insert** a **graphic** between the **PRACTICE GREEN**... and **LOOK FOR**...headings.

13. **Center** the **graphic**.

14. Size the graphic without distorting it so that it causes the document to fully fill the page.

15. Verify that it matches the outcome as shown on the following page.

PRACTICE GREEN COMPUTING

LOOK FOR THE ENERGY STAR LABEL

25% of computer systems are left on 24 hours a day

Computers account for 5% of all commercial energy consumption

The goal of the Energy Star program is to design major computer system components that use no more than 30 watts of power when turned on but not in use. If all computers in the United States met Energy Star guidelines, enough energy could be saved to power a city of six million

Computer Services

Energy Star Outcome

PRACTICE·GREEN·COMPUTING¶

LOOK·FOR·THE·ENERGY·STAR·LABEL¶

- → 25%·of·computer·systems·are·left·on·24·hours·a·day¶
- → Computers·account·for·5%·of·all·commercial·energy·consumption¶

The·goal·of·the·Energy·Star·program·is·to·design·major·computer·system·components·that·use·no·more·than·30·watts·of·power·when·turned·on·but·not·in·use.·If·all·computers·in·the·United·States·met·Energy·Star·guidelines,·enough·energy·could·be·saved·to·power·a·city·of·six·million·people·for·one·year!¶

Buy·computer·equipment·with·the·Energy·Star·logo.¶

Computer Services

Microsoft Word 2007/10

Cut & Paste and Copy & Paste

Cut & Paste is the process of MOVING text or files from one location to another. For example, if you are writing a letter using Microsoft Word. You have several paragraphs typed. After reviewing what you have typed, you decide that the 3rd paragraph would be better placed in front of the second paragraph. You can highlight the 3rd paragraph, right-click it, click cut, right-click in front of the 2nd paragraph, and click paste, That moves the 3rd in front of the 2nd.

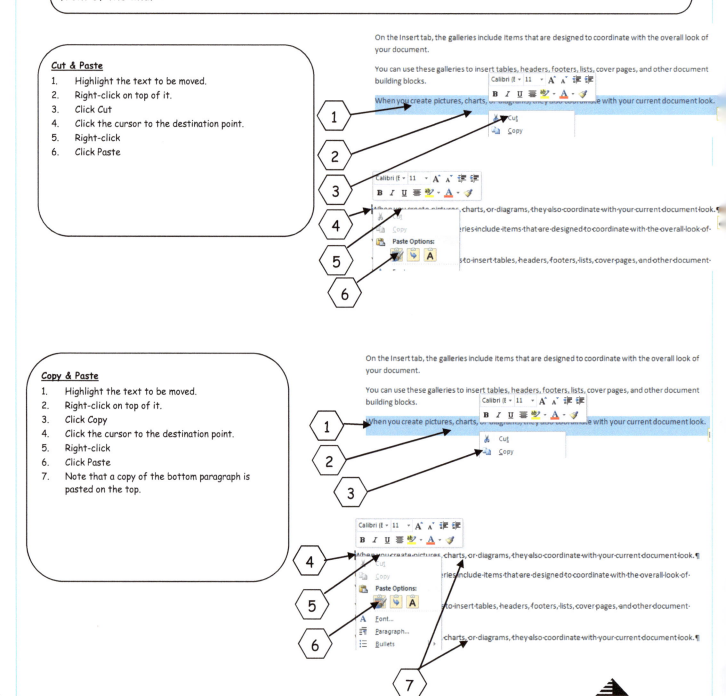

Cut & Paste
1. Highlight the text to be moved.
2. Right-click on top of it.
3. Click Cut
4. Click the cursor to the destination point.
5. Right-click
6. Click Paste

Copy & Paste
1. Highlight the text to be moved.
2. Right-click on top of it.
3. Click Copy
4. Click the cursor to the destination point.
5. Right-click
6. Click Paste
7. Note that a copy of the bottom paragraph is pasted on the top.

Computer Services